# ELIJAH,
# MESSENGER of GOD

illustrated by Leon Baxter

adapted by Diana Craig

Macdonald

Brave King Ahab ruled the land of Israel. But the mighty king had one weakness – his beautiful wife Queen Jezebel.

Jezebel came from another land where the people prayed to an evil god called Baal. When she married Ahab, she brought her priests with her – four hundred and fifty of them!

Jezebel always got her own way, for Ahab would do anything to please her. But one thing troubled Jezebel. She hadn't got a temple for Baal and her priests.

'Ahab!' she called, 'I want a temple for Baal, the finest ever built! When it's ready, your people must give up their God and pray to my Baal. Anyone who disobeys . . .' she paused and laughed wickedly, 'will be thrown to the dogs.'

Ahab hated to refuse, but this worried him. 'We'll never get away with it! My people will be furious. They'll riot!'

Jezebel's eyes flashed angrily. 'You're not afraid, are you?' she sneered. 'Who's in charge here anyway – you or those people you are supposed to rule?'

'I'm in charge, of course,' huffed Ahab, puffing out his chest. 'I'll speak to the builders at once.'

God had heard everything and he burned with anger at the wicked king. Ahab must be punished. But who would tell him? And then God remembered Elijah, the only man who could be trusted to take his message to the king.

Soon nearly everyone in Israel was forced to pray to Baal in the new temple. Ahab didn't care whom he prayed to, and anyway, he was king, and kings did whatever they liked. But Ahab had no idea God was about to send him a visitor.

God wished everyone was as good as Elijah. For Elijah knew exactly what was right and what was wrong, and he never made a false move. God had no doubts that Elijah was just the man to show the king and the others how to behave. When God explained how Ahab was leading his people astray, Elijah was beside himself with rage. He could hardly wait to see the king and, grabbing a date cake to munch on the way, he strode off towards the royal palace.

By the time he got to the palace, Elijah was quite out of breath. But, fearlessly pushing past the guards, he marched straight into the throne room. With his piercing eyes and wild hair, he looked a frightening figure. The courtiers giggled nervously at the strange man in rough clothes.

'You think you can do as you please,' declared Elijah, glaring at Ahab. 'You think you're more important than God, don't you? Well, I've got news for you. Until I say so, there'll be no more rain, not even a single dew drop.'

Ahab burst out laughing. 'You old fool! You can't scare me like that! Be off with you, before I call the guards!'

Elijah wasn't in the least bit afraid of the king, but God knew it wouldn't be safe for him to stay a minute longer in the city. So he told Elijah to go and hide near a small stream in a desert valley.

'You can drink from the stream, and every morning and evening I shall send ravens to bring you food,' said God.

Elijah wasn't quite sure how the ravens were going to feed him, but he knew God wouldn't let him down. He set off to find the lonely spot in the desert.

When he got there, Elijah made his home in a cave where he could shelter from the scorching sun. The desert all around was hot and dusty, but Elijah could wet his dry lips and quench his thirst from the sparkling stream in the valley. And sure enough, at sunrise the ravens brought him bread, and at sunset they brought him meat, just as God had promised.

With no rain to stop it drying up, the earth soon split into huge cracks. Every morning the level of the stream dropped a bit more. Soon it was no more than a trickle. And then, one day, it dried up completely! But Elijah was not worried. He knew God would not let him die.

God told Elijah what to do. 'Go to the nearest town, and you will see a woman gathering sticks. She'll take over from the ravens and shelter you.'

As Elijah approached the town gates, he saw the woman God had described. 'Please give me some water,' he asked, 'oh, and a little piece of bread, too.'

The woman was horrified. 'Bread? How can you ask me for bread?' she wailed. 'All I have is a little flour and oil, just enough for a last loaf for myself and my son. When that's gone, we must starve!'

'No, you won't,' Elijah replied confidently, 'God will make sure there's enough food for us until it rains again.'

'The poor man's been in the sun too long; he's gone mad,' the woman thought. 'I'd better take him home or there's no telling what might happen to him!'

The woman used half her flour and oil to make a loaf for Elijah, then reached for the last half to make some bread for herself and her son. But to her amazement, she found the jars were still full. And it was the same the next day, and the day after that. No matter how much flour or oil she took out, the jars were always full to the brim.

'See? I told you God would look after us,' said Elijah.

One day, the woman's son fell ill. His face was deathly white, and his mother couldn't feel a breath of life in him. Sobbing and wailing, she rushed to Elijah.

'Is this my reward for feeding you and giving you a home?' she choked through her tears. 'If you really can talk to God, ask him to bring my son back to life!'

Elijah gently took the boy from her arms, carried him upstairs and laid him on the bed. Then he prayed:

'Please God, don't make this good woman suffer. Don't let her boy die.'

The words were hardly out of his mouth when the boy began to stir, his eyelids fluttered, and a moment later he sat up.

'Where am I?' he asked, rubbing his eyes and yawning. 'Oh hello, Elijah. How long have I been asleep?'

Laughing, Elijah carried the boy back to his mother. When she saw he was alive and well again, she nearly fainted.

'It's a m-miracle!' she stammered, when at last she was able to speak. 'Thank you, Elijah, thank you!'

And all this time it still hadn't rained. Back in Israel, most of the crops had died for lack of water, and the people were starving.

Up in his palace, King Ahab was brooding. Why didn't Baal answer his prayers and send rain?

'If it doesn't rain soon, we'll have to kill some of the cattle – there isn't enough grass left for all of them,' he muttered as he paced the room. 'If only I could get my hands on that Elijah, wherever he is . . . he's at the bottom of all this!'

God knew that Ahab was at the end of his tether. He could also see how much the people were suffering. So God spoke to Elijah again: 'Go back to Ahab. It's time it rained.'

When the news of Elijah's return reached the king, Ahab was furious and rushed off to meet him. He'd show Elijah who was boss!

'You've got a nerve to show your face here, after all the trouble you've caused!' he yelled when he found Elijah.

'You're the one who's caused trouble, not me,' Elijah replied firmly. 'If you hadn't made God so angry, he wouldn't be punishing you now. Well, the drought hasn't changed your mind, but I know something that will. We'll have a contest. Then you'll see who is the real god!'

Ahab glumly agreed. He was desperate and he'd try anything. Perhaps God *could* end the drought, perhaps Baal wasn't real after all.

There hadn't been such excitement for years. Bursting with chattering curiosity, the people gathered to watch the contest. Suddenly Elijah appeared, with a face like thunder. Everyone fell silent as his voice boomed over their heads.

'Foolish people, this is your last chance! Come back to God and all will be forgiven . . . or stay with Baal and die!'

Then he explained the rules of the contest. 'The priests of Baal must build a fire to sacrifice a bull on. I'll do the same. Then the priests must pray to Baal, and I'll pray to God. Only the real god will be able to light the fire.'

Soon, a huge pile of logs towered above the priests. Slowly, they began to circle the pile, dipping and swaying in a strange dance, while waving their arms in the air.

'Oh Baal, send us fire,' they chanted over and over again . . . but nothing happened, not even a flicker of flame.

'Why don't you shout louder?' Elijah jeered. 'Perhaps Baal is too busy to hear you, or maybe he's asleep!'

Hours went by, and the dance grew wilder and wilder. By now it was getting very late. At last, one by one, the priests wearily sank to the ground. They had given up.

Now it was Elijah's turn. Carefully, he arranged twelve stones on the ground and neatly piled some wood on top of them. Then he dug a trench all the way round the fire. He told the people to pour water over the wood until it was dripping wet and the trench was flooded. And then, with his hands tightly clasped, he prayed to God.

'Everything is ready, God. Now show the people your power!'

At once, a tremendous flash of lightning snaked down from the sky and struck the top of the pile. The wood burst into a roaring flame. Everything was swallowed up in the fire – wood, stones, earth, the lot! The flames even danced on the water in the trench!

A huge gasp of amazement rose from the astonished crowd, and then everyone began to cheer and stamp and shout.

'Hooray, hooray! God is the winner! Baal has no power at all! Three cheers for Elijah!'

Elijah knew that they had seen the truth at last.

Hardly daring to look at the sky, Elijah and his servant climbed to the top of the mountain that overlooked the embers of the fire. Kneeling on the ground, with his face hidden between his knees, Elijah asked his servant:

'Can you see any rain clouds?'

'No, master, the sky is as clear as glass,' came the reply.

Six times Elijah repeated the question, and six times he got the same answer. But the seventh time, the servant came running, very excited.

'Master, master, there is a tiny cloud, no bigger than my fist!' he cried.

Elijah hurried down the mountain. 'Come on everyone, run home before you all get drenched!' he shouted with joy. 'God has forgiven you. It's going to rain!'

And with these words, the sky grew black with clouds, the wind began to howl and, with an ear-splitting crack of thunder, the rain came bucketing down. Jostling and pushing, the great crowd of people surged towards home.

'Hey, wait for me!' called King Ahab, slipping and sliding in the mud as he struggled on to his chariot.

And as for Elijah . . . well he was so overjoyed he just hitched up his cloak and ran in front of Ahab's chariot, all the way back to the city.

This story has been told in many different ways for nearly three thousand years. It was first written down in a language called Hebrew. Since then, it has been re-told in almost every language used in the world today.

    You can find the story of Elijah in the Bible. This part of his life is in the First Book of the Kings, Chapters 16 to 18.